# TAKE US
# TO YOUR
# MALL

## Other FoxTrot Books by Bill Amend

**FoxTrot**
**Pass the Loot**
**Black Bart Says Draw**
**Eight Yards, Down and Out**
**Bury My Heart at Fun-Fun Mountain**
**Say Hello to Cactus Flats**
**May the Force Be With Us, Please**

## Anthologies

**FoxTrot: The Works**
**FoxTrot** *en masse*
**Enormously FoxTrot**

# TAKE US TO YOUR MALL

## A FoxTrot Collection
## by Bill Amend

**Andrews and McMeel**
A Universal Press Syndicate Company
**Kansas City**

To Madeline

NO DEEP-SPACE METEORS CRASHING DOWN ON OUR HEADS...

NO RADIOACTIVE SPIDERS INFECTING OUR BLOOD-STREAMS...

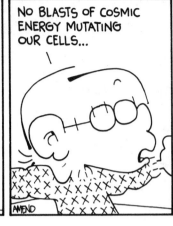

NO BLASTS OF COSMIC ENERGY MUTATING OUR CELLS...

AT THIS RATE WE'RE **NEVER** GONNA BE SUPERHEROES.

O YE OF LITTLE FAITH...

HUH-HUH, HUH-HUH, HNNGH, HUH-HUH, HUH, HNNGH...

STOP IT!

HUH-HUH, HNNGH, HUH-HUH, HUH-HUH, HNNGH...

I SAID, **CUT IT OUT!**

HUH-HUH, HNNGH...

MOM, PETER'S DOING THAT STUPID "BEAVIS AND BUTT-HEAD" LAUGH AND HE'S DRIVING ME NUTS!

PETER, GO DO YOUR HOMEWORK.

THANK YOU, MISS TATTLETALE.

HUH-HUH, HUH-HUH, HNNGH, HUH-HUH, HNNGH...

YOU TOO, PAIGE.

PAIGE HAS BEEN TAKING VITAMINS WITH IRON.

OH, MAN, IF THIS WORKS...

# FoxTrot
## BILL AMEND

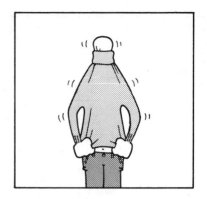

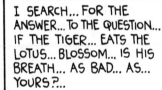

PERFECT.

I'LL ONLY ASK YOU ONCE. WHERE'S MY HOMEWORK?

OK! OK! I HID IT IN MY CLOSET!...

MOM, YOU'D BETTER LET ME MAKE MY OWN SANDWICH TODAY.

WHY'S THAT?

YOU KNOW HOW WHEN I HAVE A MATH TEST SCHEDULED I LIKE IT CUT INTO TRAPEZOIDS FOR GOOD LUCK AND WHEN I HAVE A VOCABULARY QUIZ I LIKE IT CUT INTO OVALS?

YESSS...

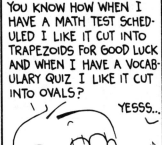

WELL, TODAY I HAVE BOTH.

I SEE.

I JUST WISH I KNEW WHAT A TRAPOVALOID LOOKED LIKE.

THERE'S A PROTRACTOR IN THE BREAD DRAWER.

MAYBE THERE'S JUST NO SUCH THING AS A FRISBEE IGUANA.

ONE MORE TRY...

ARE THESE **PAIGE'S** CDs?

# FoxTrot

## BILL AMEND

**Panel 1:**
AM I THE PERFECT ZOMBIE, OR WHAT?

YOU'RE ADORABLE. NOW GO DO YOUR HOMEWORK.

**Panel 2:**
ADORABLE?! I'M A ZOMBIE, MOTHER! I'M SUPPOSED TO BE GRUESOME!

YOU'RE RIGHT. YOU'RE GRUESOME. NOW, GO.

**Panel 3:**
YOU'RE JUST SAYING THAT! YOU THINK I'M ADORABLE! AAAAAA!

**Panel 4:**
YOU KNOW, I'M NOT SURE ZOMBIES ARE SUPPOSED TO BE QUITE SO HIGH-STRUNG.

I KNEW I SHOULD'VE SPRUNG FOR THOSE ZOMBIE TEETH DELUXE...

5TH GRADE HALLOWEEN COSTUME CONTEST

Grrr Grrr Grrr Grrr Grrr Grrr Grrr

UM, PERHAPS PRINCIPAL MARTINI WOULD LIKE TO ANNOUNCE THE WINNERS?...

OH NO, THESE ARE **YOUR** MONSTERS, MISS O'MALLEY.

AMEND

**Panel 1:**
SO HOW WAS THE COSTUME CONTEST?

PRETTY GOOD. I WON "MOST REALISTIC."

**Panel 2:**
JASON, CONGRATULATIONS! THAT'S GREAT!

IT'S OK. WHAT I **REALLY** WANTED TO WIN WAS "BEST OF SHOW," BUT I WAS DISQUALIFIED BEFORE THE FINAL JUDGING.

**Panel 3:**
WHAT FOR?

TRYING TO EAT THE VISIBLE MAN'S INNARDS.

**Panel 4:**
YOU KNOW, THE GOOD METHOD ACTORS SET LIMITS.

ANYWAY, YOU MAY GET A PHONE CALL...

AMEND

# FoxTrot
## BILL AMEND

"MARY LOU WANTS TO PLANT A FLOWER GARDEN."

"IF HER PLOT IS 8' x 10' AND THE SEEDS MUST BE SPACED AT LEAST ONE FOOT APART, WHAT IS THE LARGEST NUMBER OF SEEDS SHE CAN PLANT?"

WELL?

ZERO. IT'S NOVEMBER.

DID I MENTION HOW EXCITED I AM THAT YOU'RE PAYING ME BY THE HOUR?

I SUPPOSE SHE COULD BE LIVING IN AUSTRALIA

I HATE WORD PROBLEMS.

ARE YOU KIDDING? WORD PROBLEMS ARE GREAT!

WITHOUT WORD PROBLEMS, MATH WOULD BE JUST SOME ABSTRACT BUNCH OF FORMULAS THAT LIVE ONLY WITHIN THE CONFINES OF A CLASSROOM OR A TEXTBOOK.

BUT IN REALITY, MATH IS EVERYWHERE YOU LOOK! IT PERMEATES EVERYTHING! YOU CAN'T ESCAPE IT! AND THAT'S WHAT WORD PROBLEMS LET US IN ON.

AND THAT'S **NOT** A REASON TO HATE THEM?

AND THE MORE MATH YOU LEARN, THE MORE MATH YOU SEE...

SO WHAT DO I OWE YOU FOR ALL THIS?

LET'S SEE... THREE HOURS OF MATH TUTORING AT 75¢ PER HOUR...

THAT COMES TO $31.50.

I THINK YOU MEAN $2.25.

BRA-VO! YOU PASSED YOUR FINAL TEST! WELL DONE, PAIGE!

RATS.

# FoxTrot
## BILL AMEND

PETER FOX TAKES THE HANDOFF AND STREAKS DOWNFIELD!

WITH UNHEARD-OF SPEED, HE PUTS THE DEFENSE TO SHAME! REGGIE WHITE BOUNCES OFF! CHARLES HALEY BOUNCES OFF! DERRICK THOMAS BOUNCES OFF!

AMEND

THE KID IS AMAZING! NO ONE CAN STOP HIM!

HOMEWORK. NOW.

NO ONE EXCEPT...

MOM, CAN I HAVE SOME MONEY TO GO TO THE MOVIES?

WHAT HAPPENED TO YOUR ALLOWANCE?

I SPENT IT ALL. PLEEEASE?

PETER, THIS IS WHY PEOPLE MAKE BUDGETS. YOU HAVE TO PRIORITIZE AND LIMIT YOUR SPENDING. IF YOU REALLY WANTED TO SEE A MOVIE, YOU SHOULD HAVE SET ASIDE SOME MONEY FOR IT. I'M SORRY, BUT NO.

BUT MOM...

NO. I WANT YOU TO LEARN SOMETHING FROM THIS.

...THAT FROM NOW ON, I ASK DAD.

IS $10 ENOUGH?

AMEND

QUINCY, FETCH!

QUINCY, DON'T FETCH!

AMEND

UNREAL...

ATTA BOY!

# FoxTrot
## BILL AMEND

LET'S SEE... WHAT DO I WANT TO DO TODAY?...

I COULD PLAY COMPUTER GAMES...

I COULD SORT MY "STAR TREK" TRADING CARDS...

WAS THIS COMIC BOOK YOURS?

I COULD PLAN THE PERFECT MURDER...

AT LEAST I DIDN'T SPILL **CHOCOLATE** MILK...

WHAT ARE YOU DOING?

WRITING MURDER-MYSTERY NOVELS.

UM, IS THERE A PARTICULAR REASON **WHY**?

IT'S GREAT! I CAN DREAM UP ALL SORTS OF SINISTER CRIMES, I'LL NEVER GET IN TROUBLE, AND WITH LUCK I'LL MAKE LOTS OF MONEY.

CHECK OUT MY LIST OF POSSIBLE TITLES.

DON'T BE SO SURE ABOUT THAT "NEVER GET IN TROUBLE" PART.

I ESPECIALLY LOOK FORWARD TO WRITING "PAIGE'S MURDER ON THE ORIENT EXPRESS" AND "PAIGE'S DEATH ON THE NILE."

HEY, PAIGE — WANNA SEE THE MYSTERY NOVEL I'M WRITING?

NO.

C'MON, DON'T YOU WANT TO SEE EVEN A **LITTLE** OF IT?

NO!

PLEEEASE? ARE YOU **SURE** YOU DON'T WANT TO SEE IT?

OK, OK! I'LL LOOK AT IT!

TOUGH. IT'S TOP SECRET. BA HA HA HA HA!

SPEAKING OF MYSTERIES...

**Panel 1:**
"Press 'M' for Murder"
by Jason Fox

**Panel 2:**
Paige Fox enters her bedroom as she does every day after school. Suddenly, a 16-ton weight falls from the ceiling and squishes her dead!!!

The End

**Panel 3:**
HMM. SOMETHING'S MISSING...

**Panel 4:**
... a 16-ton weight with razor-sharp spikes...

**Panel 5:**
I HEAR YOU'RE WRITING MURDER MYSTERIES.

YUP. I'M WORKING ON MY SEVENTH ONE NOW.

**Panel 6:**
GOSH, A REGULAR J.B. FLETCHER!

WHO'S THAT?

**Panel 7:**
JESSICA FLETCHER. ANGELA LANSBURY'S CHARACTER ON "MURDER, SHE WROTE."

**Panel 8:**
I MEAN, IN TERMS OF PROLIFICACY.

It was then that the killer spotted his next victim...

**Panel 9:**
PETER SAYS THAT IN ALL YOUR LITTLE MYSTERY STORIES, **I'M** THE ONE WHO GETS MURDERED!

NOT TRUE!

**Panel 10:**
WHILE I ADMIT I KILL YOU OFF IN "PAIGE FALLS DOWN THE 39 STEPS," "PAIGE'S MURDER IN THE RUE MORGUE" AND "PAIGE'S BODY IN THE LIBRARY," IN THIS NEW ONE I'VE ACTUALLY MADE YOU THE **KILLER.**

**Panel 11:**
"PAIGE OF THE BASKERVILLES."

**Panel 12:**
THERE'S JUST NO PLEASING SOME PEOPLE.

# FoxTrot
## BILL AMEND

PETER, WHAT ARE YOU DOING?

STRETCHING MY JAW MUSCLES.

WHAT ON EARTH FOR?

I WANT TO BE ABLE TO SHOVEL IN AS MUCH FOOD AS POSSIBLE THIS THANKSGIVING. I WAS REALLY DISAPPOINTED BY MY PERFORMANCE LAST YEAR.

AMEND

YOU ATE SEVEN PLATEFULS!

MY GOAL WAS TO MATCH MY AGE.

PETER, JUST BECAUSE YOUR FATHER DOES THAT...

HE MAKES IT LOOK SO EASY.

OOO-A FRESH BLOCK OF CHEDDAR...

SO HOW GOES THE PRE-THANKSGIVING TRAINING?

PRETTY WELL. TODAY I'M TRYING TO STRETCH MY STOMACH.

HOW?

WELL, I FIGURED I'D CHUG A BUNCH OF COKE AND THEN JUMP AROUND. MY HOPE IS THAT ALL THE CARBON DIOXIDE WILL BLOW UP MY STOMACH LIKE A BALLOON.

SOUNDS DANGEROUS.

FOR MY STOMACH?

FOR ME TO STAND HERE!

BRAAAP!!

AMEND

I AM SOOOO HUNGRY...

DID YOU EAT LUNCH?

NO WAY— I'M FASTING.

WHAT?!

AMEND

TOMORROW'S THANKSGIVING. IF I DON'T STARVE MYSELF TODAY, I'LL NEVER BE ABLE TO EAT 16 HELPINGS! I JUST WISH IT WERE A LITTLE EASIER.

WHAT'S THE POINT OF BEING MISERABLE TODAY JUST SO YOU CAN EAT TOO MUCH AND BE MISERABLE TOMORROW?!

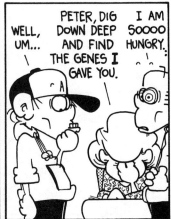

WELL, UM...

PETER, DIG DOWN DEEP AND FIND THE GENES I GAVE YOU.

I AM SOOOO HUNGRY.

**ARE WE READY TO RUMMMBLE?!...**

**DADDY, THIS IS THANKSGIVING, NOT A BOXING MATCH!**

**EVIDENTLY, YOU'VE NEVER REACHED FOR THE MASHED POTATOES AT THE SAME TIME AS PETER.**

**DIBS ON THE TURKEY.**

**DEAR LORD...**

**WELL, PETER, YOU DID IT.**

**YOU ATE YOUR AGE IN PLATEFULS OF FOOD. SIXTEEN HELPINGS OF TURKEY, STUFFING AND MASHED POTATOES... NOT TO MENTION PUMPKIN PIE.**

**I CERTAINLY HOPE YOU'RE HAPPY.**

**I WOULD BE IF I WEREN'T IN THIS COMA.**

**WHEN YOU GET A CHANCE, HELP ME LIFT YOUR FATHER OUT OF HIS CHAIR.**

**UNBELIEVABLE!**

**WHAT?**

**I ATE 16 PLATEFULS OF FOOD ON THANKSGIVING, THREE SLICES OF PIE, AND I DIDN'T GAIN ANY WEIGHT! NOT A SINGLE POUND!**

**IT'S NOT FAIR! AM I DOOMED TO BE SKINNY FOREVER?!**

**LET ME TRY ANOTHER SCALE...**

**HE EATS 16 HELPINGS AND I'M THE ONE ABOUT TO BE SICK.**

# FoxTrot
## BILL AMEND

WELL, DENISE, FOR ONCE I'M TOTALLY ON TOP OF THINGS.

I'VE RESERVED OUR LIMO FOR THE HOLIDAY FORMAL, I'VE RESERVED MY TUXEDO FOR THE HOLIDAY FORMAL, I'VE MADE OUR DINNER RESERVATIONS FOR THE HOLIDAY FORMAL...

THERE WAS SOMETHING I STILL NEEDED TO DO... WHAT WAS IT?

ASK ME TO **GO** WITH YOU, MAYBE?

OH, YEAH—WHAT KIND OF CORSAGE DO YOU WANT?

PETER, I CAN'T BELIEVE YOU'VE MADE ALL THESE PLANS FOR THE HOLIDAY FORMAL!

WHY?

YOU HAVEN'T EVEN ASKED ME TO **GO** WITH YOU!

OH.

I MEAN, JUST BECAUSE I'M YOUR GIRLFRIEND DOESN'T MEAN YOU CAN TAKE ME FOR GRANTED! TALK ABOUT **INSULTING**! I'M NOT **ALWAYS** A SURE THING, YOU KNOW!

OK, OK, I'M SORRY. DENISE, WILL YOU GO TO THE DANCE WITH ME?

YES. BUT UNDER PROTEST.

NOW, THEN, OUR DINNER RESERVATIONS ARE FOR 7:30.

HI, PETER? IT'S ME, DENISE.

YO. WHAT'S UP?

I JUST FOUND OUT THAT MY PARENTS ARE TAKING ME UP TO VISIT MY GRANDMOTHER THE SAME WEEKEND AS THE HOLIDAY FORMAL.

CAN'T YOU GET OUT OF IT?

WELL, SHE'S KINDA GETTING UP THERE IN YEARS. I THINK IT'S PROBABLY JUST A LITTLE MORE IMPORTANT FOR ME TO SPEND TIME WITH HER THAN TO GO TO A DANCE.

OH.

EVEN A DANCE WITH **ME**?

AS HARD AS THE CONCEPT MIGHT BE FOR YOU TO GRASP...

AAAA! WHY DOES THIS SORT OF THING ALWAYS HAPPEN TO ME?!

WHAT?

DENISE BAGGED ON THE HOLIDAY FORMAL! MY OWN GIRLFRIEND! I'M DATELESS!

SO?

SO?! I'VE GOT A LIMO LINED UP... DINNER LINED UP... A TUXEDO LINED UP... A CORSAGE LINED UP... ALL OF IT WASTED! IT'S NOT LIKE I CAN JUST TAKE SOMEBODY ELSE!

MONOGAMY STINKS.

SPEAKING AS A NOGAMIST...

AMEND

I HEAR DENISE CAN'T GO TO THE BIG DANCE WITH YOU.

THANK YOU, BLABBER-MOUTH PAIGE!

IT'S NOT THE END OF THE WORLD, PETER. THERE'LL BE OTHER DANCES.

I KNOW, BUT I HAD THIS ONE ALL PLANNED! NOW I HAVE TO CANCEL THE LIMO CANCEL THE FLORIST, CANCEL THE TUXEDO... IT'S A TOTAL PAIN IN THE REAR!

MAYBE YOU COULD TAKE SOMEONE ELSE?

ARE YOU KIDDING? I'D DIE!

YOUR FEELINGS FOR DENISE ARE THAT STRONG?

HER TANTRUMS ARE.

AMEND

PETER, I HAVE TO GO VISIT MY GRANDMOTHER. I'M SORRY.

SO I'M SUPPOSED TO GO TO THIS DANCE BY MYSELF?!

BE STILL MY HEART.

MINDY, DON'T EVEN THINK IT.

AMEND

27

# FoxTrot

## BILL AMEND

29

# FoxTrot
## BILL AMEND

Dear, Dear, Dear,

Dear, Dear, Dear, Dear, Dear, Dear, Dear, Dear, Dear, Dear,

Dear Santa,

For Christmas this year, I'd like the following:

A tarantula,

A boa constrictor,

And a large, gray rat.

I hope you'll come through for me. I'd be the happiest kid alive.

Sincerely, Paige Fox

SMEAR SOME CLEARASIL ON IT FOR ADDED REALISM.

WHAT ARE YOU SMURFS UP TO?

31

I'M TOTALLY DEAD. I'M TOTALLY DEAD. I'M TOTALLY DEAD.

PETER, WHAT'S WRONG?

YOU KNOW HOW DENISE CAN'T GO TO THE FORMAL WITH ME BECAUSE SHE HAS TO GO VISIT HER GRANDMOTHER?

YESSS...

WELL, NOW THIS OTHER GIRL, MINDY, HAS ASKED ME TO GO WITH HER AND IF I **DO**, DENISE WILL BE CRUSHED AND IF I **DON'T**, THIS MINDY GIRL WILL BE.

...OR SO YOU ASSUME.

HEY— WE'RE TALKING PETER FOX.

GOSH, TOO BAD THERE AREN'T **TWO** OF YOU.

I KNOW WHAT SOLOMON WOULD SUGGEST...

OK, THIS IS IT. HEADS, I GO WITH MINDY TO THE FORMAL; TAILS, I DON'T.

BOINK BOINK

DOESN'T COUNT. IT LANDED ON A CRUMB.

WILL YOU JUST MAKE UP YOUR MIND?!

SO, UM, DO YOU THINK YOU'LL GO TO THE DANCE WITH ME?

MINDY, UM, SEE... HERE'S MY PROBLEM...

I, UM, WELL, I HAVE A GIRLFRIEND. I MEAN, I'VE BEEN GOING OUT WITH DENISE FOR OVER A YEAR NOW AND, WELL, I THINK IT WOULD REALLY HURT HER IF I WENT WITH SOMEONE ELSE TO THE FORMAL. I'M SORRY.

BUT SHE BLEW YOU OFF! SHE LEFT YOU DATELESS! IT'S HER OWN FAULT THAT YOU'RE UP FOR GRABS!

MINDY, THE POINT IS THAT I'M NOT UP FOR GRABS.

AT LEAST NOT FOR MY GRABS, APPARENTLY.

MINDY, I WISH THERE WERE SOMETHING I COULD **DO**, BUT...

HEY, PETE, AREN'T YOU GOING TO INTRODUCE ME?

MINDY, YOU'LL GET OVER ME SOMEDAY, I'M SURE OF IT.

YOU MAY NOT THINK SO NOW, YOU MAY NOT THINK SO TOMORROW, BUT EVENTUALLY YOU'LL FORGET ALL ABOUT STUPID PETER FOX AND HOW MUCH HE HURT YOU.

YOU JUST GOTTA HANG IN THERE, KIDDO. BROKEN HEARTS DO HEAL.

ARE YOU LISTENING TO ME?

...SO THEN AFTER THE DANCE, I THOUGHT MAYBE WE COULD GO OUT FOR ICE CREAM...

I KNOW JUST THE PLACE...

UNBELIEVABLE. IT'S UNNNN-BELIEVABLE.

WHAT IS?

YOU KNOW HOW I'VE BEEN GOING NUTS ALL WEEK TRYING TO FIGURE OUT WHAT TO DO ABOUT THIS GIRL WHO ASKED ME TO THE FORMAL?

YEAH, SO?

WELL, ALONG COMES MY FRIEND STEVE, I INTRODUCE THEM, AND KAPOW, THEY'RE IN LOVE. I MEAN GA-GA CITY. NOW HE'S GOING TO THE DANCE WITH HER. IT'S SIMPLY UNBELIEVABLE!

THAT YOUR IMPOSSIBLE SITUATION ACTUALLY WORKED OUT?

THAT HER CRUSH ON ME COULD BE SO FLEETING.

STILL, YOUR EGO SEEMS UNSCATHED.

PETER, I'M SORRY I WAS SUCH A CRY-BABY ABOUT ALL THIS.

DENISE, DON'T WORRY ABOUT IT.

IT'S JUST THAT THE THOUGHT OF YOU POSSIBLY GOING TO THE HOLIDAY FORMAL WITH ANOTHER GIRL, WELL, IT KINDA RIPPED ME UP INSIDE.

I KNOW. I'M SORRY. I PROBABLY SHOULD'VE BEEN MORE MINDFUL OF YOUR FEELINGS.

AT LEAST THINGS WORKED OUT FOR EVERY-BODY.

STEVE'S TAKING MINDY TO THE DANCE AND PAYING ME FOR THE LIMO DEPOSIT, YOU GET TO VISIT YOUR GRANDMOTHER WITHOUT HAVING TO WORRY ABOUT ME, AND I GET TO SPEND SATURDAY NIGHT HERE AT HOME.

OK... FOR ALMOST EVERY-BODY.

JASON, I SAID LATER.

"SUPER MARIO UNIVERSE 2" AWAITS...

# FoxTrot
## BILL AMEND

34

MOM, CAN YOU KEEP AN EYE ON QUINCY FOR A WHILE?

WHAT FOR?

I'M WRAPPING CHRISTMAS PRESENTS IN MY ROOM AND I DON'T WANT HIM TO SEE WHAT I GOT HIM.

AMEND

OF ALL THE TIMES TO BE LEFT SPEECHLESS.

YOU CAN FEED HIM SOME CRICKETS IF HE BEHAVES HIMSELF.

WOW! I CAN'T BELIEVE DAD GOT ME A BEAVIS STOCKING!

I CAN'T BELIEVE DAD GOT ME A BUTT-HEAD ONE!

HUH-HUH HUH-HUH M HUH HNNGH M HNNGH HUH M HUH-HUH-HUH M HUH-HUH HUH-HUH M HUH HNNGH HUH HUH-HUH HUH HUH M HUH HNNGH HUH M HUH-HUH

**THEY** CAN'T BELIEVE IT?!?

THE WOMAN AT THE STORE SAID THEY WERE QUITE THE RAGE.

LET ME SHOW YOU RAGE.

AMEND

DID YOU SEE THE MISTLETOE I PUT UP?

WHAT'S WITH ALL THESE MAGAZINES?

AMEND

I TELL YOU, THERE'S NOTHING WORSE THAN GOING SHOPPING TWO DAYS BEFORE CHRISTMAS...

...AT THE LARGEST MALL IN TOWN...

...WITH PAIGE.

EXCEPT MAYBE GOING ONE DAY BEFORE CHRISTMAS. GOD FORBID. HEY, PETER—WHAT ARE YOU DOING TOMORROW?

DAD, WE NEED A FAX MACHINE. WHY'S THAT?

WELL, I'VE GOT THIS LAST-MINUTE ADDENDUM TO MY CHRISTMAS LIST AND IT'S TOO LATE TO GET IT TO SANTA ANY OTHER WAY. IF WE HAD A FAX, I'D BE ALL SET.

ALSO, IF WE HAD ONE, I COULD SEND NEAT-O CARTOONS AND MESSAGES TO YOU AT WORK EVERY DAY.

I'D LIKE TO RETURN THIS, IF POSSIBLE. I THOUGHT YOUR WIFE REALLY WANTED ONE.

FAXMASTER 550

TO A MERRY CHRISTMAS, EVERYONE!

EEW! WHAT'S IN THIS EGGNOG?!

WHOOPS. THAT WAS MEANT FOR PAIGE.

LET'S SEE... SALAD FORK OR DINNER FORK?

...AND A MORE PEACEFUL NEW YEAR.

# FoxTrot
## BILL AMEND

HEY, PETER— WANNA DRIVE ME TO THE MALL?

WHAT FOR?

I WANT TO BUY A VIDEO GAME CARTRIDGE WITH MY CHRISTMAS MONEY.

WHICH GAME?

I'D RATHER NOT SAY. I'D HATE FOR YOU TO GET IN TROUBLE WITH MOM AND DAD FOR BEING A KNOWING ACCESSORY TO THIS PURCHASE.

AMEND

OF COURSE, THAT ALONE TELLS ME TOO MUCH.

LET'S JUST SAY V-GAMER DIGEST GAVE IT FOUR SEVERED THUMBS UP.

SALE!!! ALL SEGA & NINTENDO CARTRIDGES 0.5% OFF!

I CAN'T BELIEVE I'M ACTUALLY THE PROUD OWNER OF "MORTAL KARNAGE II."

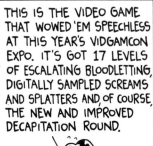

THIS IS THE VIDEO GAME THAT WOWED 'EM SPEECHLESS AT THIS YEAR'S VIDGAMCON EXPO. IT'S GOT 17 LEVELS OF ESCALATING BLOODLETTING, DIGITALLY SAMPLED SCREAMS AND SPLATTERS AND, OF COURSE, THE NEW AND IMPROVED DECAPITATION ROUND.

VIOLENCE UNMATCHED ANYWHERE.

ARE YOU TALKING ABOUT THE GAME OR MOM'S LIKELY REACTION?

HEY, IF THIS WERE SO BAD FOR KIDS, THEY WOULDN'T SELL IT TO KIDS, RIGHT?

AMEND

C'MON, POP IT IN.

PETER, YOU CAN'T PLAY A GAME OF "MORTAL KARNAGE II'S" COMPLEXITY WITHOUT FIRST READING THE INSTRUCTION MANUAL.

LET'S SEE... TO THROW A BASIC PUNCH, HOLD DOWN THE "B," "C" AND "X" BUTTONS, TAP THE "START" BUTTON, USE THE ARROW PAD TO INDICATE DIRECTION AND RELEASE THE "C" BUTTON WHEN THE FORCE BAR TOPS 80 PERCENT.

AMEND

MORTAL KARNAGE II

THAT'S A **BASIC** PUNCH?!

WHOOPS. THAT WAS AN UPPER-CUT. THE BASIC PUNCH DOESN'T USE THE "X" BUTTON.

ALREADY THIS GAME IS MAKING REAL-LIFE FIGHTING SEEM ATTRACTIVE.

HERE'S A FOLD-OUT CHART SHOWING HOW TO KICK...

OK, I'M ENTERING THE TEMPLE OF THE DRAGON LORD...

NOW, IF A NINJA SHOWS UP, I HAVE TO RIGHT AWAY DOUBLE-CLICK ON THE "A" BUTTON TO RIP HIS THROAT OUT...

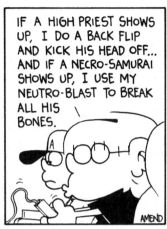

IF A HIGH PRIEST SHOWS UP, I DO A BACK FLIP AND KICK HIS HEAD OFF... AND IF A NECRO-SAMURAI SHOWS UP, I USE MY NEUTRO-BLAST TO BREAK ALL HIS BONES.

WHAT IF MOM SHOWS UP?

HIDE THE CARTRIDGE AND LIE LIKE A RUG. WHY?

JASON, WHAT'S THIS?

MOM, WHAT ARE YOU DOING?!

TAKING AWAY THIS VIDEO GAME CARTRIDGE, FOR STARTERS.

BUT YOU CAN'T! I BOUGHT IT WITH MY CHRISTMAS MONEY! IT'S MINE!

JASON, I TOLD YOU TWO WEEKS AGO THAT I DIDN'T WANT "MORTAL KARNAGE II" COMING INTO THIS HOUSE. YOU HAVE NO ONE TO BLAME BUT YOURSELF.

BUT... BUT...

YOU'RE TOO YOUNG FOR THIS SORT OF THING. I MEAN, LOOK AT WHAT IT TEACHES: THAT HUMAN DISEMBOWELMENT IS ENTERTAINMENT... THAT "WINNERS" DECAPITATE THEIR ENEMIES... THAT CARNAGE IS SPELLED WITH A "K"...

I KNOW CARNAGE ISN'T SPELLED WITH A "K."

THE SAD PART IS, THAT'S THE LEAST OF MY CONCERNS.

MOM, I'VE GIVEN IT SOME THOUGHT, AND YOU'RE RIGHT— I'M TOO YOUNG FOR A VIDEO GAME LIKE "MORTAL KARNAGE II."

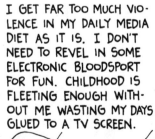

I GET FAR TOO MUCH VIOLENCE IN MY DAILY MEDIA DIET AS IT IS. I DON'T NEED TO REVEL IN SOME ELECTRONIC BLOODSPORT FOR FUN. CHILDHOOD IS FLEETING ENOUGH WITHOUT ME WASTING MY DAYS GLUED TO A TV SCREEN.

JASON, THOSE ARE VERY MATURE OBSERVATIONS. I'M IMPRESSED.

MATURE ENOUGH TO GET ME BACK MY "MORTAL KARNAGE II" CARTRIDGE?

CAN'T BLAME ME FOR TRYING.

OH, YES I CAN.

# FoxTrot
## BILL AMEND

PAIGE MUST BE COOKING DINNER.

I'LL GO OPEN A WINDOW.

DINER EST SERVI!

WE'RE JUST GONNA EAT CEREAL.

NO WAY, BUCKOS. JUST BECAUSE MOM AND DAD ARE GONE DOESN'T MEAN YOU CAN EAT FROOT LOOPS FOR DINNER!

I SLAVED ALL AFTERNOON MAKING THIS MEAL AND YOU'RE GOING TO EAT IT!

NOW, THEN, DO YOU WANT A LOT OF SPAGHETTI OR A LITTLE SPAGHETTI?

CHUNK! CHUNK! CHUNK!

THAT'S **SPAGHETTI**?!?

OH, WAIT— THIS IS THE PEACH COBBLER.

I THINK WE HAVE HERE THE MAKINGS OF A KILLER WEIGHT-LOSS PROGRAM.

EMPHASIS ON "KILLER."

TWEEE!

RELAX— IT'S JUST THE SMOKE ALARM.

AMEND

# FoxTrot
## BILL AMEND

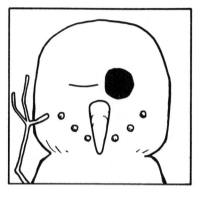

# FoxTrot
## BILL AMEND

**Panel 1:** MOM, I HAVE TO WRITE AN ESSAY ON "MACBETH" AND I THOUGHT MAYBE YOU COULD HELP ME WITH IT.
"MACBETH"? YOU'RE STUDYING "MACBETH"?

**Panel 2:** "IS THIS A DAGGER WHICH I SEE BEFORE ME, THE HANDLE TOWARD MY HAND?... I GO, AND IT IS DONE; THE BELL INVITES ME. HEAR IT NOT, DUNCAN; FOR IT IS A KNELL THAT SUMMONS THEE TO HEAVEN OR TO HELL!"

**Panel 3:** THAT "MACBETH"?

**Panel 4:** I KEEP FORGETTING YOU WERE AN ENGLISH MAJOR.
ACT I. SCENE I.— AN OPEN PLACE. THUNDER AND LIGHTNING. ENTER THREE WITCHES...

**Panel 5:** MOM, LOOK, "MACBETH" MAY GET **YOU** ALL EXCITED, BUT TO ME IT'S JUST A PLAY.
JUST A PLAY?!

**Panel 6:** JUST A PLAY?!

**Panel 7:** ONE OF SHAKESPEARE'S GREATEST AND DARKEST AND RELEVANT TRAGEDIES AND YOU CONSIDER IT JUST A **PLAY**?!

**Panel 8:** OK, A PLAY AND A SPIT SHIELD.
DID YOU BREAK THAT BINDING?

**Panel 9:** ANYWAY, I KINDA HOPED YOU COULD HELP ME WITH THIS "MACBETH" ESSAY I HAVE TO WRITE.
HAVING TROUBLE COMING UP WITH A GOOD THESIS?

**Panel 10:** HAVING TROUBLE COMING UP WITH KEY EXAMPLES SUPPORTING YOUR THESIS?

**Panel 11:** HAVING TROUBLE WRAPPING IT ALL UP WITH A STRONG AND CLEAR CONCLUSION?

**Panel 12:** UM, WHAT'S "MACBETH" ABOUT?
IT'S ABOUT 100 PAGES. NOW GET GOING.

WELL, IT'S TAKEN TWO DAYS...

THREE HOURS AND 28 MINUTES...

BUT I'VE FINALLY FINISHED...

...READING PAGE ONE.

YOU KNOW, THEY CAN PERFORM THESE PLAYS IN TWO HOURS...

I FINISHED READING "MACBETH"... I FINISHED READING "MACBETH"...

NOW I CAN START WRITING MY ESSAY...

TALK ABOUT MOOD SWINGS.

AND IT'S DUE IN 14 HOURS.

MOM, CAN YOU HELP ME WITH MY "MACBETH" ESSAY?

PAIGE, WE'VE BEEN THROUGH THIS ALL WEEK!

I'M NOT GOING TO TELL YOU WHAT THE PLAY IS ABOUT! I'M NOT GOING TO BUY YOU THE CLIFFS NOTES! I'M NOT GOING TO TELL YOU WHAT TOPIC TO CHOOSE AND I'M NOT GOING TO WRITE HALF YOUR SENTENCES FOR YOU! I'M SORRY! THE POINT OF THIS ASSIGNMENT IS FOR **YOU** TO DO THE WORK!

JUST DOUBLE-CHECK MY SPELLING.

WHY DIDN'T YOU JUST **SAY** SO?

I LIKE TO WATCH YOUR CHEW-OUTS FALL FLAT.

PAIGE, HOW DO YOU SPELL "MACBETH"?

# FoxTrot
## BILL AMEND

47

# FoxTrot
## BILL AMEND

MOM, CAN YOU HELP US SETTLE AN ARGUMENT? WHO'S THE COOLEST OF THE X-MEN — CYCLOPS OR WOLVERINE?

WOLVERINE. DEFINITELY.

HA! SEE?!

NOW LET ME WORK.

YOUR MOM'S PRETTY COOL.

FOR A MOM.

ROGER, OUT OF CURIOSITY, WHO THE **HECK** ARE THE X-MEN?

HMM?

MMM — HONEY, THIS IS DELICIOUS!

I MEAN, THE SAUCE IS OUT OF THIS WORLD!

BOY, IS THIS A FAR CRY FROM THE LASAGNA YOU **USED** TO MAKE!

DAD, THIS IS TAKEOUT.

I MEAN, UM, "A FAR CRY" IN THE DIFFERENT-BUT-EQUALLY-YUMMY SENSE...

THE REAL QUESTION IS HOW DOES YOUR **FOOT** TASTE?

HEY, PAIGE, HAPPY GROUNDHOG DAY.

AAAA!

SORRY. I DIDN'T HAVE A GROUNDHOG.

SUDDENLY, I WISH IT WERE ARMISTICE DAY...

THAT'S NOT TILL NOVEMBER, PAL.

PETER, I WAS MAKING YOUR BED TODAY AND GUESS WHAT I FOUND UNDER YOUR MATTRESS?...

MOM, I CAN EXPLAIN!

I JUST HAVE THOSE MAGAZINES FOR THE ARTICLES! I **SWEAR!**

I WAS TALKING ABOUT YOUR NEW BASEBALL MITT.

OH, UM, THAT'S HOW YOU BREAK IT IN.

NOW, WHAT'S THIS ABOUT MAGAZINES?

YOU MEAN MY SCIENTIFIC AMERICAN COLLECTION?...

AMEND

ICK. HOW CAN YOU EAT THAT STUFF?

SUGAR-FROSTED HONEY FLAKES?

THEY'RE NOTHING BUT SUGAR AND ARTIFICIAL CHEMICALS! I MEAN, LOOK AT YOUR MILK—IT'S TURNED INTO SOME PURPLISH OOZE!

IT IS PRETTY DISGUSTING.

SO THEN WHY DO YOU EAT SIX BOWLS OF IT EVERY MORNING?!

FOR THE GLOW-IN-THE-DARK DINOSAUR STICKERS.

ACTUALLY, I'M A LITTLE SURPRISED THAT **YOU** DON'T GLOW IN THE DARK BY NOW.

IN ANOTHER MONTH, I'LL HAVE WALLPAPERED MY ROOM.

AMEND

LET'S GO, GUYS. IT'S PAST YOUR BEDTIME.

BUT... BUT...

NO "BUTS." LET'S GO. UPSTAIRS.

BUT "BLOOD ZOMBIES FROM PLANET X" JUST **STARTED!** WE CAN'T TURN IT OFF **NOW!**

OH, YES YOU CAN.

BUT WE JUST DRANK A SIX-PACK OF COLA. EACH.

WELCOME TO THE **REAL** LATE-NIGHT TELEVISION WAR.

PLEASE? PLEASE? PLEASE? PLEASE? PLEASE? PLEASE? PLEASE? PLEEEEEEEEASE?

AMEND

A THREE POINTER AT THE BUZZER...

IT'S GOOD! HOLY COW! THEY WIN!

YES! YES! YES! YES! YES! YES! YES! YES! YES! YES! YES!

HOO BOY, AM I WINDED.

YOU KNOW, WHEN YOU'RE NOT EVEN IN GOOD ENOUGH SHAPE TO **WATCH** BASKETBALL...

AEROBICS?! ME?! ARE YOU CRAZY?!

IT'LL BE GOOD FOR YOU.

AEROBICS?! ME?! ARE YOU CRAZY?!

ROGER, YOU'RE TOTALLY OUT OF SHAPE. FACE IT.

AEROBICS?! ME?! ARE YOU CRAZY?!

WE'LL GO TOGETHER. IT'LL BE FUN.

HELLOOOO, SPANDEX...

I **MUST** BE CRAZY.

HI, YOU MUST BE NEW. I'M TINA, YOUR AEROBICS INSTRUCTOR.

HI... I'M... ROGER...

HEE HEE... FORGIVE ME IF... I'M A LITTLE OUT OF BREATH... IT'S BEEN A... WHILE SINCE I'VE DONE ANY REAL... EXERCISE...

I GUESS YOU COULD SAY... I'M A TAD OUT OF... SHAPE...

CERTAINLY CONSIDERING THAT WE HAVEN'T EVEN **STARTED**.

I KINDA JOGGED UP THE FRONT STAIRS.

HERE'S SOME MORE WATER.

...AND IN CASE ANYONE WAS WORRIED, YES, I **DO** KNOW CPR.

PHEW.

PHEW.

PHEW.

ANDY, WHY ARE THEY ALL LOOKING AT ME?

JUST SAY "PHEW," ROGER.

OK, EVERYONE, BEFORE WE BEGIN THE AEROBICS, LET'S DO A LITTLE STRETCHING.

YAWN

YAWN

THEY PROBABLY ADDED THIS PART FOR THESE EARLY-MORNING CLASSES.

ROGER, DEAR, I'M PRETEND-ING I DON'T KNOW YOU.

I'D SAY MY FIRST ATTEMPT AT AEROBICS WENT RATHER WELL...

WOULDN'T YOU AGREE?

ARE YOU JOKING?

YOU WERE A NIGHTMARE! YOU DIDN'T DO ANY OF THE MOVES RIGHT, YOU KEPT KNEEING ME IN THE THIGH, I'M COVERED WITH BRUISES AND TO TOP IT ALL OFF, YOU SANG ALONG TO THE MUSIC! I AM **NEVER** TAKING YOU AGAIN!

...RATHER WELL, INDEED...

I MEAN, YOU COULDN'T HAVE BEEN MORE OBNOXIOUS IF YOU'D **TRIED!**

I SWEAR, IF JASON DOESN'T START CLEANING UP HIS ROOM...

WHAT'S THIS?

Dear Gretchen,
I think you're the prettiest girl in the school. Please be my valentine.
Love,
Jason

DID ANYONE ELSE JUST HEAR A LOUD "THUD"?

JASON WROTE A **LOVE** LETTER?!

I SAW IT ON HIS DESK! IT WAS ADDRESSED TO SOMEONE NAMED GRETCHEN!

IT SAID HE THOUGHT SHE WAS THE PRETTIEST GIRL IN THE SCHOOL AND HE ENDED IT "LOVE, JASON." NOW, WHAT DO **YOU** CALL THAT?!

THE END OF AN ERA...

OUR BABY'S GROWING UP...

IT SEEMS LIKE JUST YESTERDAY HE WAS CALLING GIRLS "REPUL-SOIDS" AND "BOOG-O-TRONS."

ACTUALLY, IT WAS THIS MORNING.

WELL, I'VE GONE THROUGH JASON'S YEARBOOK FROM LAST YEAR AND I CAN'T FIND A SINGLE GIRL NAMED GRETCHEN.

OF COURSE, THAT DOESN'T MEAN SHE COULDN'T BE NEW THIS YEAR, OR MAYBE GRETCHEN IS A MIDDLE NAME OR SOMETHING.

I SUPPOSE I COULD CALL THE SCHOOL AND HAVE THEM CHECK THEIR RECORDS. WHAT DO YOU THINK?

WHY DON'T YOU JUST ASK **JASON** WHO SHE IS?

AND HAVE HIM THINK I'M **NOSEY?!**

53

MOM, WHAT'S WRONG?

OH, I'M JUST FLOUNDERING IN ONE OF MY USUAL PARENTAL DILEMMAS.

A FEW DAYS AGO, I STUMBLED ACROSS A VALENTINE'S DAY CARD THAT JASON HAD WRITTEN TO SOME GIRL AT HIS SCHOOL NAMED GRETCHEN. IT WAS, SHALL WE SAY, OF A ROMANTIC NATURE.

JASON?! THIS IS JASON?!

ANYWAY, I'M DYING TO FIND OUT MORE ABOUT THIS GIRL, BUT I DON'T DARE TELL HIM THAT I—...

JASON AND GRETCHEN, SITTIN' IN A TREE...

...KNOW.

WHO TOLD YOU ABOUT GRETCHEN?

JASON, SWEETIE, I SAW THE VALENTINE'S DAY CARD YOU MADE FOR HER.

IT'S PRETTY OBVIOUS THAT YOU LIKE HER A LOT, AND I JUST WANT YOU TO KNOW THAT IT'S OK. NO ONE IS GOING TO MAKE FUN OF YOU.

I JUST WISH YOU'D TELL US ABOUT HER.

WELL, SHE HAS THIS GREAT WAY OF EATING MICE...

DID YOU SAY MICE?

ARE WE ALLOWED TO MAKE FUN OF GRETCHEN?

GRETCHEN'S A SNAKE?!

SHE'S MISS O'MALLEY'S BOA CONSTRICTOR.

YOU MADE THAT VALENTINE'S DAY CARD FOR A SNAKE?!

WHO'D YOU THINK IT WAS FOR?

WELL, FOR STARTERS, A GIRL.

EEW! GROSS! ICK! WHAT KIND OF A WEIRDO DO YOU THINK I AM?!

DON'T ASK.

WOULD IT BE OK IF MARCUS AND I BUILT AN ANDROID THIS WEEKEND?

# FoxTrot
## BILL AMEND

DG JQZLF RGLP HQIR?

PETER, WHAT ARE YOU DOING?

GQLMN BDOG SNGM.

WHAT?!

KRMLVR BLMQ ZMSOLN.

WHAT?!

GETTING IN SHAPE FOR BASEBALL SEASON.

AS THRILLED AS I AM THAT YOU'RE ONLY CHEWING GUM...

JASON, MOVE IT. I HAVE TO WRITE A PAPER.

TOUGH. I'M PLAYING "IRON MYSTICUS."

WHAT'S THAT?

IT'S THIS COOL NEW CD-ROM COMPUTER GAME. YOU ROAM AROUND AN ALIEN WORLD FINDING CLUES AND SOLVING PUZZLES WHILE BEING STALKED BY A KILLER ROBOT.

WHEN WILL YOU BE DONE?

HARD TO SAY. A GAME LIKE THIS MIGHT GO ON FOREVER.

GUESS NOT.

HEY! WHAT HAPPENED TO MY "PAIGE'S HOMEWORK" FOLDER?!

SIGH.

SHE'S LOOKING AT ME!

SHE'S LOOKING AT ME!

SHE'S LOOKING AT ME!

SHE'S LOOKING AT ME!

BURP.

# FoxTrot
## BILL AMEND

JASON FOX IS OUR NEXT $10 MILLION WINNER!!!

I WON $10 MILLION! I WON $10 MILLION! I'M RICH! I'M RICH! I WON $10 MILLION!

ODD THAT THEY WOULD SEND SUCH IMPORTANT NEWS VIA BULK RATE MAIL.

LOOK, QUINCY— "JASON FOX IS OUR NEXT $10 MILLION WINNER"!

I'M RICH! I'M RICH! I'M FILTHY, STINKING RICH!

I CAN'T BELIEVE I WON THE SWEEPSTAKES! I CAN'T BELIEVE THEY REALLY PICKED ME!

ESPECIALLY SINCE I CAN'T RECALL EVER SENDING IN AN ENTRY.

MOM! LOOK! I WON $10 MILLION!

SEE?! IT SAYS SO ON THE ENVELOPE: "JASON FOX IS OUR NEXT $10 MILLION WINNER"!

IMAGINE ALL THE WONDERFUL THINGS THIS MONEY WILL LET ME DO!

I THINK I'LL GO LAUGH IN MY UGLY SISTER'S FACE.

I'VE GOT TO GET AN OFFICE OUTSIDE OF THIS HOUSE.

I CAN'T BELIEVE I ACTUALLY WON $10 MILLION!

I SUPPOSE AT THIS POINT I SHOULD FIND MYSELF A GOOD FINANCIAL ADVISER.

SOMEONE WITH EXPERIENCE HANDLING LARGE BLOCKS OF MONEY...

GLAD YOU COULD COME OVER, MR. $5-A-WEEK ALLOWANCE.

WHAT'S THE EMERGENCY?

YOU KNOW, I'LL BET I'M THE FIRST KID FROM OUR SCHOOL TO WIN A $10 MILLION DRAWING.

HEY—YOU NEVER OPENED THE ENVELOPE.

I WAS TOO EXCITED. IT'S PROBABLY JUST FULL OF LEGAL FORMS AND INSTRUCTIONS ON HOW TO PICK UP MY MONEY. LET'S TAKE A LOOK...

RIP RIP RIP

JASON FOX IS OUR NEXT $10 MILLION WINNER!!!

...IF ENTRY NUMBER X10J7680T3 IS SELECTED IN OUR SWEEPSTAKES DRAWING.

MAYBE I SHOULD TELL IBM TO PUT A HOLD ON THAT ORDER...

YOU MIGHT ALSO WANT TO CALL BACK THAT REALTOR LADY...

MOM, I JUST FOUND OUT I DIDN'T WIN $10 MILLION AFTER ALL.

I KNOW, SWEETIE. I'M SORRY.

I THOUGHT FOR SURE I HAD. I MEAN, THE ENVELOPE SAID, "JASON FOX IS OUR NEXT $10 MILLION WINNER." ISN'T THAT LYING?

THEY CALL IT MARKETING.

IF YOU KNEW I DIDN'T WIN, WHY DIDN'T YOU TELL ME?

YOU WERE SO HAPPY, I FIGURED IT COULDN'T HURT TO LET YOU THINK YOU WERE A MILLIONAIRE FOR A FEW HOURS.

UM...

WHAT DO YOU MEAN BY "UM"?

MOM, THERE'S A HERSHEY TRUCK BACKING INTO OUR DRIVEWAY!

# FoxTrot
## BILL AMEND

I WILL NOT BE IGNORED.

I SAID...

HEY, PAIGE— LOOK...

JASON, WILL YOU GO **AWAY**?!

YOU WOULDN'T SPEAK TO ME LIKE THAT IF YOU WEREN'T SO MUCH OLDER THAN ME.

IN FACT, I HAVE A GOOD MIND TO STICK YOU ON A ROCKET SHIP FOR A 5-YEAR, ROUND-TRIP FLIGHT AT 0.98 TIMES THE SPEED OF LIGHT.

WHERE, ACCORDING TO EINSTEIN'S THEORY OF SPECIAL RELATIVITY, YOU WOULD AGE ONLY ONE YEAR TO MY FIVE HERE ON EARTH.

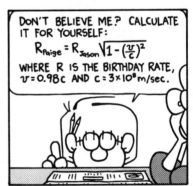

DON'T BELIEVE ME? CALCULATE IT FOR YOURSELF:

$$R_{Paige} = R_{Jason} \sqrt{1 - \left(\frac{v}{c}\right)^2}$$

WHERE R IS THE BIRTHDAY RATE, $v = 0.98c$ AND $c = 3 \times 10^8$ m/sec.

THAT WOULD MAKE US BOTH 15. EQUALS.

YESSIREE, I HAVE A GOOD MIND TO DO JUST THAT.

BUT FOR NOW, I'LL GO AWAY...

WHAT I WOULDN'T **GIVE** FOR A SPACESHIP.

HEY, PETER— WANNA DRIVE MARCUS AND ME OUT TO THE MINIATURE GOLF COURSE?

SURE. YOU BET. I'D LOVE TO.

LET ME GET MY CAR KEYS.

...BUDDY.

THOSE MUST'VE BEEN **SOME** PHOTOS YOU TOOK OF HIM AND HIS GIRLFRIEND.

BRING YOUR WALLET TOO, BIG GUY.

THE THING I LIKE MOST ABOUT MINIATURE GOLF IS IT'S SUCH A GREAT EQUALIZER.

THERE'S SO MUCH LUCK INVOLVED THAT EVEN A SPAZ LIKE ME HAS A CHANCE OF MAKING A HOLE-IN-ONE.

THE, UM, HOLE'S OVER THERE...

OK, SO IT'S A **SLIM** CHANCE.

I GUESS NOW WE KNOW HOW THE SPHINX LOST ITS NOSE.

WAS MY FORM OK?

# FoxTrot
## BILL AMEND

WHO WANTS COFFEE?

ME!

ME!

ME!

THEN I'LL GO MAKE SOME.

NEVER MIND.

NEVER MIND.

NEVER MIND.

MOM, HOW DO YOU USE THE NEW COFFEE MAKER?

WELL, LET'S SEE... FIRST YOU MAKE SURE EVERYTHING'S CLEAN...

THEN YOU PUT A FILTER IN THE BASKET... MEASURE OUT THE GROUND COFFEE INTO THE FILTER...

PUT THE BASKET BACK INTO ITS SLOT, POUR YOUR WATER INTO THE TOP AND HIT THE "ON" SWITCH.

IT'S REALLY PRETTY SIMPLE.

EEW! PAIGE, WHAT IS THIS?!

GO BACK TO THAT PART ABOUT A FILTER...

YOU KNOW, WE DO HAVE "INSTANT"...

AMEND

**MOM! MOM! I'M GOING TO BE WORKING ON THE SCHOOL NEWSPAPER!**

**PAIGE, THAT'S GREAT!**

**I'LL BE DOING A "QUESTION WOMAN" COLUMN WHERE I GO AROUND AND GET STUDENTS' OPINIONS ON VARIOUS TOPICS.**

**OOO...**

**NO LONGER WILL I SIMPLY BE "PAIGE FOX, ANONYMOUS FRESHMAN"... FROM NOW ON I'LL BE "PAIGE FOX, ALL-POWERFUL QUESTION WOMAN"! THIS IS SO EXCITING!**

**FOR ONCE I'LL BE TAKEN SERIOUSLY.**

**UM, ABOUT THE HAT...**

**LET'S SEE... I THINK WE'VE JUST ABOUT COVERED EVERYTHING.**

**YOU'RE FOR U.S. MILITARY INTERVENTION IN BOSNIA, AGAINST CONTINUED DEFICIT SPENDING BY CONGRESS AND AGAINST USING THE DEATH PENALTY ON MINORS.**

**CORRECT.**

**NOW FOR THE TOUGH ONE...**

**IF YOU WERE ON A DESERT ISLAND AND COULD HAVE ONLY ONE FAST FOOD RESTAURANT...**

**HMMMMMM...**

**WOULD YOU MIND IF I POLLED YOU ON A FEW THINGS FOR THE SCHOOL NEWSPAPER?**

**UM...**

**UM...**

**UM...**

**NEXT!...**

**COULD YOU REPEAT THE QUESTION?**

# FoxTrot
## BILL AMEND

MOM, I WANT A DOG.

A DOG.

A BIG DOG. LIKE A GERMAN SHEPHERD OR A DOBERMAN. ONE WITH LOTS OF TEETH.

IS THERE A REASON?

HEY, MOM — GUESS WHO'S PLAYING "WEENIE MAN" AT THE SCHOOL NUTRITION FAIR?!

AND I WANT IT TODAY.

PAIGE, NO.

THE SECRET OF A GOOD PAPER AIRPLANE IS IN THE WEIGHT DISTRIBUTION.

ALL RIGHT, WHO THREW — THAT?!

THAT AND USING SOMEONE ELSE'S OLD HOMEWORK.

HUGH ANDREWS, I'D LIKE TO SEE YOU AFTER CLASS.

I CAN'T **TELL** YOU HOW GREAT MY DAY WAS, ANDY!

GOOD.

# FoxTrot
## BILL AMEND

AH, SPRING.

I LOVE THE SOUNDS, THE FRESH WARM AIR, THE EXPLOSION OF COLORS... DOES THIS SEASON EVEN **HAVE** A DOWNSIDE?

I HAD TO ASK.

WHO WANTS TO PLAY CATCH?

JASON, IT'S EASY.

I THROW THE BALL, YOU WATCH THE BALL, YOU SWING THE BAT, YOU HIT THE BALL.

HERE WE GO.

I GUESS I SHOULD'VE ADDED "HOLD ON TO THE BAT."

MAYBE **YOU** SHOULD WEAR THE HELMET.

FASTBALL!

DING!

SCREWBALL!

DING!

KNUCKLEBALL!

DING!

I THINK I NEED A NEW MASK.

YOU KNOW, YOU **DO** HAVE A GLOVE...

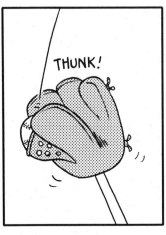

# FoxTrot
## BILL AMEND

**Panel 1:**
WHAT ARE YOU PLAYING?

THIS NEW COMPUTER GAME, "PRINCE OF ASSYRIA."

LOOKS PRETTY GORY.

*Slash Slash*

**Panel 2:**
DEFINITELY. IT'S ONE OF THOSE GAMES WHERE YOU HAVE TO BE FAST OR YOU'RE DEAD.

*Slash Whap Slash*

**Panel 3:**
WRITING YOUR REPORT? GOOD FOR YOU!

In conclusion,

**Panel 4:**
AND FAST YOU ARE.

WHY, THANK YOU.

*Slash Whap*

AND TO THINK I USED TO WONDER IF I WAS UNDERPAID.

I TAKE IT WE WEREN'T SUPPOSED TO SHAKE THE VIAL THAT SAID, "DO NOT SHAKE."

EEGAD! MY PANTS ARE DISSOLVING!

$\frac{\Delta P}{\Delta T}$

$6 \cdot 10^{23}$

**Panel 1:**
MR. FOX, THERE'S A DAN DALTON HERE TO SEE YOU.

YOU'VE GOT TO BE KIDDING ME.

**Panel 2:**
THAT GUY'S THE BIGGEST PAIN IN THE REAR I'VE EVER MET. TELL HIM I'M OUT. TELL HIM I'M IN A MEETING. TELL HIM TO TAKE HIS STUPID SALES PITCH TO WHERE THE SUN DOESN'T SHINE.

**Panel 4:**
AND PLEASE TELL ME YOU'RE USING THE HANDSET AND NOT THE SPEAKERPHONE...

UM...

WHY DON'T I TELL HIM...

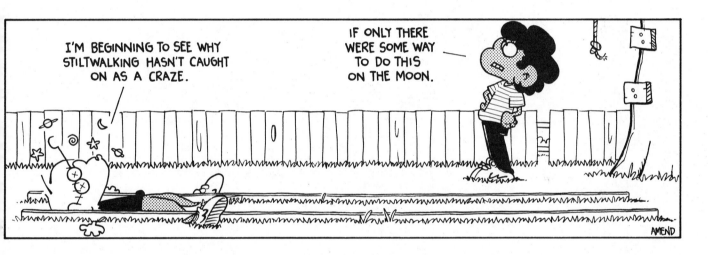

# FoxTrot
## BILL AMEND

Dear Diary,

It's time I told the truth. It's time I came clean.

I'm really a space alien.

I only pretend to be human. In reality, I am a loathsome, tentacled, squid-like creature.

One look at my true face would kill anyone with eyeballs. I'm that ugly.

I also eat my boogers.

"SLAM!" PAIGE, WHAT'S WRONG?

OOO, THAT BILLY WEIR— WHO DOES HE THINK HE IS?!

I'VE NEVER FELT SO LOW AND HUMILIATED! SOMEONE NEEDS TO EXPLAIN TO HIM THAT NOT **EVERY** GIRL AT SCHOOL **WANTS** TO BE HIS LITTLE LOVE TOY!

DID HE MAKE INDECENT ADVANCES?

NO. HE RESISTED MINE. LIKE HE COULD DO BETTER!

YOU'LL BE WANTING NEW BOOK COVERS AGAIN, I TAKE IT.

---

LET'S SEE... I NEED A LOAF OF BREAD...

A PACK OF BOLOGNA... A PACK OF SALAMI... TWO PACKS OF CHEESE— ONE AMERICAN, ONE SWISS...

MUSTARD... MAYONNAISE... AND A HEAD OF LETTUCE.

SHOPPING LIST?

PETER'S SANDWICH INSTRUCTIONS.

WE'RE OUT OF CEREAL AGAIN.

---

♪ MACHO, MACHO MAN... ♪ I WANT TO BE... ♪ A MACHO MAN...

MACHO, MACHO MAN... ♪ I WANT TO BE... ♪ A MACHO MAN...

I WISH I HADN'T TOLD YOU THAT I HATE THAT SONG.

YOU'RE LUCKY WE DON'T KNOW MORE VERSES.

IS IT "MACHO" OR "NACHO"?

77

# FoxTrot
## BILL AMEND

YOU LOOK EXCITED.

I AM. I'M WORKING ON A BOOK REPORT.

YOU'RE ALL SMILES OVER A BOOK REPORT?!

MY TEACHER GAVE ME PERMISSION TO DO MINE AS A MULTIMEDIA COMPUTER PRESENTATION.

IT'S GOING TO BE THE GREATEST BOOK REPORT EVER. IT'LL HAVE SOUND, ANIMATION, DIGITIZED VIDEO COMMENTARY AND I HAVE AN IDEA FOR A REALLY COOL POINT-AND-CLICK HIERARCHICAL INTERFACE.

SO WHAT'S THE BOOK?

I FORGET. WANNA SEE MY FLOWCHART?

AMEND

YOU'RE DOING A BOOK REPORT ON "OLD YELLER" AND YOU HAVEN'T EVEN READ IT?!

I'M SURE I'LL GET AROUND TO IT EVENTUALLY.

EVENTUALLY.

RIGHT NOW MY BIGGEST PRIORITY IS GETTING THROUGH ALL THESE COMPUTER MANUALS.

Binary Search Trees in C J.D. Parker

AMEND

I WANT MY MULTIMEDIA BOOK REPORT TO BE THE GREATEST AND COOLEST AND MOST AMAZING BOOK REPORT MY SCHOOL HAS EVER WITNESSED.

HAVE YOU EVER BEEN HIT OVER THE HEAD WITH A SUGGESTION?

WHAT DO YOU THINK ABOUT USING THE MUSIC FROM "STAR WARS" FOR THE CREDITS?

OLD YELLER

PHEW.

IT'S TAKEN TWO DAYS OF NON-STOP WORK AND A COUPLE HUNDRED PAGES OF READING...

AMEND

...BUT I'VE FINALLY DONE IT.

I GOT THE BOOK TITLE TO DANCE ACROSS THE SCREEN.

YOU KNOW, MAYBE THERE'S A **REASON** MOST KIDS DON'T DO MULTIMEDIA BOOK REPORTS.

WHAT ARE YOU DOING?

I'M CREATING A MULTIMEDIA BOOK REPORT FOR SCHOOL.

I'VE SPENT ALL WEEK PROGRAMMING THIS THING. IT'S GOT MUSIC... IT'S GOT ANIMATION... IT'S GOT SOUND EFFECTS GALORE... IT'S GOT WIPE EFFECTS THAT'LL KNOCK YOUR SOCKS OFF...

IT'S GOT EVERYTHING.

EXCEPT A REPORT ON THE BOOK...

LOOK HOW I GOT THE END CREDITS TO SPARKLE.

THAT CONCLUDES MY INTERACTIVE MULTIMEDIA PRESENTATION ON "OLD YELLER." ANY QUESTIONS?

I HAVE JUST ONE.

ABOUT HOW I GOT THE TEXT TO DANCE ACROSS THE SCREEN? ABOUT THE COMPRESSION ALGORITHM I USED FOR THE SOUND RESOURCE FILES?

ABOUT HOW I USED THE RAM CACHE TO SPEED UP THE ANIMATION?

DID YOU EVER READ THE BOOK?

I GUESS IF YOU WANT TO GET TECHNICAL...

JASON, SEE ME AFTER CLASS. NEXT UP WILL BE SOPHIA...

HOW'D YOUR BOOK REPORT GO?

LOUSY.

IT SEEMED TOTALLY LOST ON MISS O'MALLEY WHAT A GROUND-BREAKING ACHIEVEMENT MY MULTIMEDIA PRESENTATION REPRESENTED! SHE DIDN'T CARE ABOUT MY ANIMATION... SHE DIDN'T CARE ABOUT MY CLEVER PROGRAMMING TECHNIQUES...

ALL **SHE** CARED ABOUT WAS WHETHER OR NOT I'D ACTUALLY **READ** STUPID "OLD YELLER"!

WHICH, OF COURSE, YOU **HADN'T**.

I MEAN, TALK ABOUT MISSING THE FOREST FOR THE TREES!

# FoxTrot
## BILL AMEND

DID YOU KNOW THAT THURSDAY IS TAKE YOUR DAUGHTER TO WORK DAY?

YEAH.

YOU SHOULD TAKE PAIGE.

I DON'T KNOW. I WAS THINKING IT MIGHT BE KIND OF EMBARRASSING.

Cartoonist to Pilot Mars Expedition

TO HAVE HER AROUND?

TO HAVE HER DISCOVER HOW PATHETIC MY JOB REALLY IS.

GOOD POINT.

YOU COULD DISAGREE A LITTLE...

AMEND

YO, TOADFACE...

MY NAME IS PAIGE.

Beach Hunks

YO, SQUIDLIPS...

MY NAME IS PAIGE.

Beach Hunks

YO, PAIGE...

MUCH BETTER. NOW WHAT DO YOU WANT?

AMEND

THWAP!

WHAT HAPPENED TO ALL THE COFFEE I JUST MADE?!

I, UM, DRANK IT.

YOU DRANK A WHOLE POT OF COFFEE?!

WE HAVE A BIG STAFF MEETING THIS MORNING.

AMEND

THERE'S NOTHING MORE EMBARRASSING THAN FALLING ASLEEP DURING ONE OF PEMBROOK'S ENDLESS SERMONS.

Cartoonist cast in "Sirens II"

UM, I'LL BE RIGHT BACK...

FOX, THAT'S YOUR FOURTH TRIP TO THE BATHROOM THIS HOUR!

# FoxTrot
## BILL AMEND

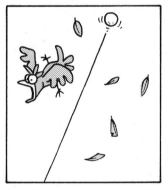

WELL, MOM, I FIGURED OUT HOW I'M GONNA MAKE MY MILLIONS.

OH? AND HOW IS THAT?

INVESTING IN COMMODITIES.

COMMODITIES.

I HEARD SOMEONE COULD MAKE, LIKE, A 10,000 PERCENT RETURN IN A YEAR. EVEN IF I DID JUST **HALF** THAT WELL I'D BE A JILLIONAIRE IN NO TIME! IT'S INCREDIBLE! HOW CAN I GO WRONG?!

AMEND

BY THE WAY, WHAT IS A COMMODITY?

JASON, WHEN YOU'RE AT SCHOOL, DO YOU GET A SENSE THAT OTHER KIDS ARE DIFFERENT?

DAD, DO YOU KNOW ANYTHING ABOUT INVESTING IN COMMODITIES?

SORT OF...

THE BASIC IDEA BEHIND COMMODITIES TRADING IS THAT YOU'RE TRYING TO PREDICT WHETHER SOMETHING WILL BECOME MORE SCARCE AND THUS **MORE** VALUABLE, OR LESS SCARCE AND THUS **LESS** VALUABLE.

AMEND

FOR EXAMPLE, IF YOU THOUGHT SPACE ALIENS WERE GOING TO COME AND TAKE AWAY HALF THE WORLD'S COWS, YOU MIGHT WANT TO LOAD UP ON CATTLE FUTURES, SINCE THE LOW SUPPLY WOULD SEND THEIR VALUE THROUGH THE ROOF.

SPACE ALIENS? THIS IS COOLER THAN I THOUGHT.

CONVERSELY, IF YOU KNEW SOMEONE WAS ABOUT TO DISCOVER A GIANT PIRATE CAVE FILLED WITH **GOLD**...

WELL, I'VE GOT MY $5 READY TO INVEST...

I'VE GOT THE BASIC PRINCIPLES OF COMMODITY TRADING ALL FIGURED OUT.

AMEND

NOW ALL I NEED IS A GOOD FINANCIAL ADVISER.

GIVE IT UP, JASON.

AT LEAST LET ME **LOOK** FOR ONE...

I'M **BEING** ONE.

WHAT ARE YOU DOING?

TRYING TO FIGURE OUT WHICH COMMODITY I WANT TO INVEST IN.

THERE ARE JUST SO MANY. THERE'S SOYBEANS... OIL... GOLD... COFFEE... WHEAT... PORK BELLIES...

EEW! DID YOU SAY PORK BELLIES?! GROSS! I'M GONNA THROW UP!

UM, WHY ARE YOU CIRCLING IT?

PAIGE, PASS ME THAT PHONE BOOK, WILL YOU?

MOM, I NEED TO BORROW SOME MONEY.

WHAT FOR?

SO I CAN INVEST IN THE COMMODITIES MARKET AND MAKE MY FORTUNE.

I THOUGHT YOU HAD $5 SAVED UP FOR THAT.

I CALLED A BROKER. THEY REQUIRE $10,000 UP FRONT. WHAT DO YOU SAY?

I HATE THAT LAUGH.

I'LL PAY YOU A DOLLAR TO MOW THE FRONT LAWN...

I HEARD YOU'VE GIVEN UP TRYING TO PLAY THE COMMODITIES MARKET.

NOT ENTIRELY.

WHILE I CAN'T AFFORD TO INVEST WITH A BROKER, I FIGURE I CAN STILL BUY AND SELL COMMODITIES ON MY OWN. ON A MUCH SMALLER SCALE, OF COURSE.

SO WHAT SORT OF COMMODITIES ARE YOU BUYING?

RIGHT NOW I'M RATHER BULLISH ON HO·HOS.

DOES PAIGE KNOW YOU HAVE THESE?

WHY DO YOU THINK I'M BULLISH?

OK, OK, I'LL PAY ANY PRICE...

# FoxTrot
## BILL AMEND

AAARGH!

PAIGE, WHAT'S WRONG?

THERE'S THIS BOY IN MY BIOLOGY CLASS WHO'S TOTALLY CUTE AND I KNOW HE LIKES ME...

BUT HE WON'T ASK ME TO THE DANCE BECAUSE HE'S TOO SHY! LIKE I'D REALLY SAY NO!

SO WHY DON'T YOU ASK HIM?

BECAUSE I'M TOO SHY.

YOU KNOW, I CAN ALREADY TELL YOU'D MAKE QUITE A COUPLE.

ASK ME TO THE DANCE.

ASK ME TO THE DANCE.

ASK ME TO THE DANCE.

ASK ME TO THE DANCE.

ASK ME TO THE DANCE.

ASK ME TO THE DANCE.

I GUESS THERE'S ALWAYS TOMORROW.

OW!

WHAT'S THE MATTER?

I GOT A PAPER CUT.

HERE, LET ME SEE...

HE'S HOLDING MY HAND! THIS IS THE MOMENT!...

I'M HOLDING HER HAND! THIS IS THE MOMENT!...

ASK ME TO THE DANCE!

# FoxTrot
## BILL AMEND

# FoxTrot
## BILL AMEND

WHERE ARE MOM AND DAD AGAIN?

AT DAD'S COLLEGE REUNION.

OH, YEAH.

IT'S HIS 25TH.

SOUNDS THRILLING.

I THINK DAD JUST WANTED TO GO SEE HOW FAT AND BALD ALL HIS CLASSMATES HAVE GOTTEN.

I WANT TO GO HOME.

TUBBY O'BRIEN— YOU'RE A TWIG! AND THAT HAIR!

CAN YOU BELIEVE IT'S BEEN 25 YEARS?!

NOPE. NOT AT ALL.

I MEAN, IT SEEMS LIKE JUST YESTERDAY WE WERE ALL STANDING HERE AT FRESHMAN ORIENTATION INTRODUCING OURSELVES TO EACH OTHER.

YESSIREE...

YUP, YUP...

TED WHITEHEAD.

ROGER FOX.

SO, FRANK...

I'M ROGER.

SO, ROGER... HOW YA BEEN?

GREAT, RICK, AND YOU?

I'M LARRY.

GREAT, LARRY, AND YOU?

THIS PLACE SURE BRINGS BACK MEMORIES, DOESN'T IT?!

SAY, WEREN'T WE ROOMMATES?

ROGER FOX? YES...

THE ROGER FOX FROM DELTA THETA HOUSE? YES...

I CAN'T BELIEVE I'VE FINALLY CAUGHT UP WITH YOU AFTER 25 YEARS!...

PIG. UH-OH. ROGER FOX?

EEGAD— IT'S MY OLD GIRLFRIEND, ANNETTE. WHERE?

OVER BY THE BAR. GO SAY HI TO HER.

ARE YOU **INSANE**?! ROGER, IT'S BEEN 25 YEARS. ANDY, THIS WOMAN WAS CRAZY ABOUT ME! I BROKE HER HEART! I SHATTERED HER UNIVERSE! MY SAYING HELLO MIGHT BE VERY, VERY PAINFUL!

ROGER **WHO**? ...VERY, VERY, **VERY** PAINFUL. MORE BEER, MISTER?

WELL, ANDY, I LIVED THROUGH MY COLLEGE REUNION. MMM.

SURE, THERE WERE GUYS WITH MORE HAIR THAN ME... GUYS WITH THINNER WAISTS. CLASSMATES WITH BETTER CAREERS...

BUT I'LL TELL YOU ONE THING— NOBODY HAD A PRETTIER **WIFE** BY HIS SIDE. ♪ THANK YOU, ROGER.

...EXCEPT DICK WILSON. WOO! ROGER, WOULD YOU LIKE TO LIVE **BEYOND** YOUR COLLEGE REUNION?...

# FoxTrot
## BILL AMEND

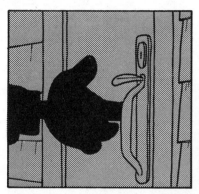

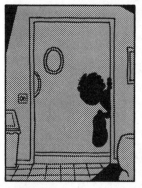

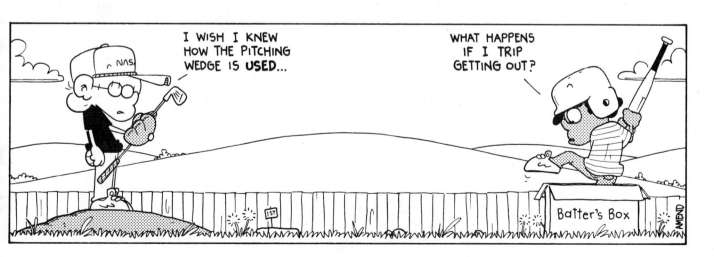

# FoxTrot
## BILL AMEND

PAIGE, C'MON, WAKE UP! GITCHY GITCHY GOO...

ZZZZ...

DAHN'T BE SILLÉE— MAGIC CARPETS ALWAYS TICKLE YOUR FEET WHEN THEY FLY.

OOO— PIERRE...

PAIGE FOX, WHAT DOES A PERSON HAVE TO **DO** TO WAKE YOU UP?!?

ZZZZ...

BREAKFAST EN BED, MA SWEET?

OOO— PIERRE...

CHOCOLAT

Le Connoisseur 512

PAIGE, I'VE TRIED TO WAKE YOU UP EVERY WAY I KNOW HOW.

ZZZZ...

REASON DIDN'T WORK... FIRMNESS DIDN'T WORK... SCREAMING DIDN'T WORK...

I DON'T KNOW WHAT ELSE I CAN DO!

ZZZZ...

...WHICH IS WHY I'M LETTING JASON TAKE OVER.

I'M UP! I'M UP! I'M UP!

NO FAIR!

# FoxTrot
## BILL AMEND

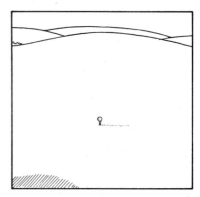

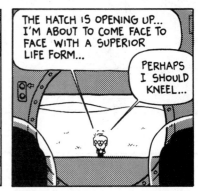

HEY, MOM! LOOK WHAT I GOT!

WHAT IS IT?

IT'S A STEALTH BLACKJACK X-220 MODEL ROCKET KIT!

IT TOOK ME 17 WEEKS TO SAVE UP THE MONEY TO BUY IT, BUT IT'S WORTH IT! ISN'T IT GREAT?! ISN'T IT INCREDIBLE?! I CAN'T WAIT TO LAUNCH IT!

WHAT DO YOU SUPPOSE THEY MEAN BY "FAA CLEARANCE REQUIRED"?

JASON, YOU KNOW THE NEIGHBORS ARE **JUST** STARTING TO SPEAK TO US AGAIN..

Stealth Blackjack X-220 Model Rocket Kit

Pre-Assembly Notes

In addition to the supplies and materials included with this kit, the following items are recommended for optimal construction and launch of the rocket:

Ruler
White glue
Art Knife
Pencil...

..."FIRE EXTINGUISHER"?!.."HIGH-PRESSURE WATER SOURCE"?!.. "COMPREHENSIVE LIABILITY INSURANCE"?!..

DO WE HAVE THEM OR NOT?

PETER, ARE YOU GONNA BE BUSY LATER TODAY?

WHY?

I THOUGHT MAYBE WE COULD GO FOR A DRIVE.

WHAT FOR?

I'M BUILDING A HIGH-PERFORMANCE MODEL ROCKET AND I WANTED TO DO SOME WIND TUNNEL TESTS BY HOLDING IT OUT THE WINDOW OF A FAST-MOVING CAR.

HOW FAST-MOVING?

WELL, LET'S SEE... IN TERMS OF KILOMETERS PER SECOND...

JASON, DO YOU REMEMBER HOW ANGRY I WAS WHEN YOU **ALMOST** GOT ME ARRESTED?

# FoxTrot
## BILL AMEND

107

# FoxTrot
## BILL AMEND

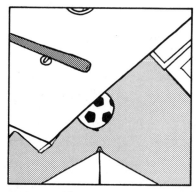

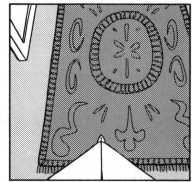

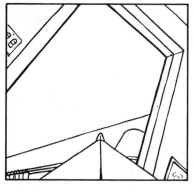

I JUST LOVE SHOPPING AT THIS STORE.

THEY'VE GOT THE BEST STUFF... THE BEST SERVICE...

...THE BEST RETURN POLICY...

I'LL NEED YOUR MOTHER'S CREDIT CARD AGAIN.

GLUG GLUG GLUG

BRAAAP!

"GUT REACTION: A PERFORMANCE PIECE BY JASON FOX." THANK YOU... THANK YOU...

SOME PEOPLE SEEM TO HAVE NO RESPECT FOR THE ARTS.

IS IT JUST ME, OR IS THE TERM "INFORMATION SUPERHIGHWAY" TOTALLY INAPPROPRIATE?

HUH?

I MEAN, SUPERHIGHWAYS WERE A PRODUCT OF THE 1950s AND '60s. THEY REPRESENT THE TRANSPORTATION TECHNOLOGY OF THE PAST.

A HIGH-SPEED DIGITAL COMMUNICATIONS NETWORK DESERVES A MORE FORWARD-LOOKING METAPHOR! ONE THAT CONJURES UP IMAGES OF THE TRANSPORTATION OF TOMORROW!

"THE INFORMATION WORM HOLE"...

IS IT JUST ME, OR HAS THIS SUMMER GONE ON TOO LONG ALREADY?

THE RAVEN SINGS AT SUNSET. IN PARIS, THE CAFÉS ARE MANY.

DEEP CAVERNS ARE KNOWN TO ECHO. THE HEAVY FLAG FLAPS NOT AT NIGHT.

ROSES COME IN MANY COLORS. THE LOCAL TRAIN STOPS ON THE HOUR.

THEY'RE ON TO US. OVER AND OUT.

HEY, PAIGE— WANT SOME LEFTOVER STEW? NO.

HOW 'BOUT SOME COTTAGE CHEESE? NO.

SOME RIPE BLACK OLIVES? NO.

JASON, I SAID TO THROW **AWAY** THE MOLDY FOOD IN THE FRIDGE! MOM, I'LL BE AT NICOLE'S.

I WILL... EVENTUALLY.

GOT ANY THREES? NO. GOT ANY FIVES?

NO. GOT ANY SIXES? NO. GOT ANY JACKS?

NO. GOT ANY EIGHTS? NO. GOT ANY TWOS?

GO **FISH**, YOU MORONS! GO **FISH**!

PAIGE, PLEASE. WE'RE HAPPY PLAYING CARDS. I'LL ASK AGAIN... GOT ANY FIVES?

# FoxTrot
## BILL AMEND

# FoxTrot
## BILL AMEND

ROGER, WOULD YOU GO WAKE UP PAIGE?

PETER, WOULD YOU GO WAKE UP PAIGE?

JASON, WOULD YOU GO WAKE UP PAIGE?

HOW IS THIS MY FAULT?!

WHEN DO YOU NEED THIS?

YESTERDAY.

WHEN DO YOU NEED THIS?

YESTERDAY.

WHEN DO YOU NEED THIS?

YESTERDAY.

SEEING AS NO ONE NEEDS ANYTHING TODAY...

I LOVE THIS TV SHOW. IT'S GOT EVERYTHING.

STUFFY BRITISH ACCENTS... REALLY BORING STORIES... WASHED-OUT COLOR...

...A PERFECT TIME SLOT...

AAAA! WHAT ARE YOU WATCHING?! "MELROSE" IS ON!

So, Denise, do you want to go out tonight?

I dunno. Do **YOU** want to go out tonight?

I dunno. Do you want to go out tonight?

I dunno. Do **YOU** want to go out tonight?

Peter, you've been on the phone for over three hours! May I use it at some point?! Please?!

Actually, why wait till tonight?...

At least let me finish breakfast.

So, Paige, I take it Jason sat behind you at the movie.

How'd you know?

HARPERS

Is it ok if Marcus and I sleep out in the living room tonight?

No way.

How 'bout up in the attic?

No way.

How 'bout down in the basement?

No way.

How 'bout in a tent out in the backyard?

**THAT** I'll consider.

You know, it's not like we **KNEW** there was a skunk in that bush!

Paige, is Peter back with that tomato juice yet?

# FoxTrot
## BILL AMEND

 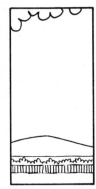

 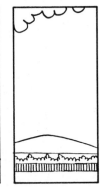  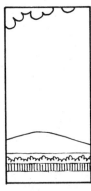  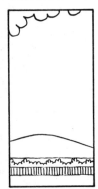

 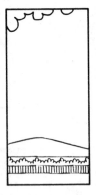

 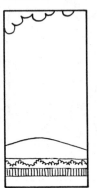

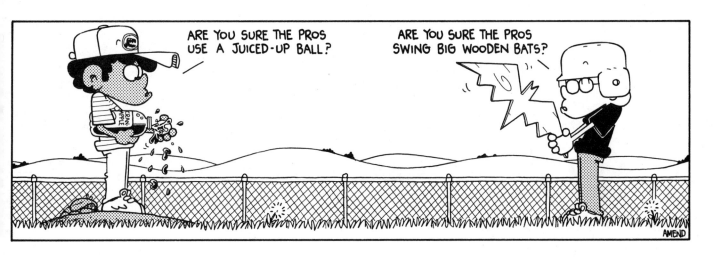

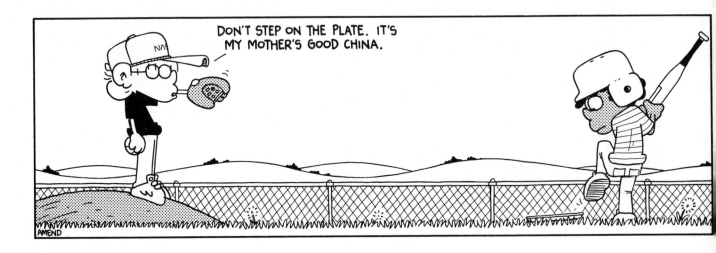

# FoxTrot
## BILL AMEND

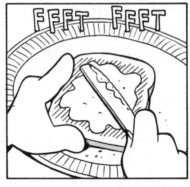

ANDY, WHAT'S THE MATTER? OH, I GUESS TURNING 42 HAS ME A LITTLE DEPRESSED.

WITH 40 AND 41, I FELT LIKE I WAS JUST A HAIR OUT OF MY 30s. BUT 42 PUTS ME SOLIDLY INTO MY 40s. MIDDLE AGE CENTRAL.

THINK ABOUT IT — I'M PRACTICALLY 45! DO YOU KNOW HOW SCARY THAT IS?!

SEEING AS I'M ABOUT TO TURN 46... OK, BAD EXAMPLE...

ROGER, I WAS THINKING...

I'M 42... YOU'RE 45... PRETTY SOON PETER'LL BE OFF TO COLLEGE... WE'RE BOTH NOT GETTING ANY YOUNGER...

Cartoonist to Judge O.J. Trial

LET'S HAVE ANOTHER KID.

I SHOULD POINT OUT THAT MY **HEART** IS ALSO 45. THE COUPLE HAD A BABY IN "FOR BETTER OR FOR WORSE"...

ANDY, WHY ON **EARTH** WOULD YOU WANT TO HAVE A BABY?! I DUNNO. I THOUGHT IT MIGHT BE FUN.

"FUN"?! "**FUN**"?! THAT'S WHAT DREAMY-EYED YOUNG COUPLES SAY, NOT 40-SOMETHING MOTHERS WITH THREE HALF-GROWN KIDS! WHAT ARE YOU THINKING?!

...NOT THAT OUR KIDS **AREN'T** LOTS OF FUN.

MOM, JASON BOOBY-TRAPPED THE TOILET AGAIN.

...IT'S JUST THAT THEY'RE **SUFFICIENT** FUN. WE COULD DO IT **RIGHT** THIS TIME...

ANDY, I DON'T MEAN TO BE STUBBORN, BUT WE'VE ALREADY **GOT** THREE KIDS!

I KNOW. YOU'RE RIGHT.

I GUESS I'M JUST A LITTLE PANICKY ABOUT MY AGE. I MEAN, I'M **42**, ROGER! IT'S LIKE MY LIFE IS SLIPPING RIGHT BY! I DON'T **WANT** TO FEEL OLD! I DON'T **WANT** TO FEEL LIKE A HAS-BEEN!

BUT WOULDN'T YOU AGREE THAT HAVING A BABY ISN'T SOMETHING ONE SHOULD DO OUT OF **PANIC**?

MAYBE I'LL JUST GET A FERRARI.

IS THE CRIB STILL UP IN THE ATTIC?

RED... WITH LEATHER...

DAD, WHAT'S WRONG?

AAAA!

IT'S YOUR MOTHER. SHE'S HAVING SOME SORT OF MID-LIFE CRISIS.

FIRST SHE WANTED TO HAVE A BABY, THEN SHE WANTED TO GET A FERRARI, NOW SHE—...

PAIGE AND I ARE OFF TO LOLLAPALOOZA.

IS THIS HER CRISIS OR **YOURS**?

AAAA!

IT'S FUNNY, ROGER.

HERE I WAS ALL WEEK FLIPPING OUT ABOUT MY AGE WHEN ALL I HAD TO DO WAS GO TO A LOLLAPALOOZA CONCERT WITH PAIGE, AND—

YOU SUDDENLY FELT YOUNG AGAIN?

NO — I WAS THRILLED **NOT** TO BE.

**PLEASE** CAN I GET A NOSE RING??

SO NO MORE MID-LIFE CRISIS?

I STILL WOULDN'T MIND A FERRARI...

FADE IN:

Opening credits.

Trumpet fanfare.

JASON FOX
PRESENTS

---

FADE TO BLACK.

FADE IN:

EXTERIOR—A&M TOXIC WASTE CO.

Ominous music.

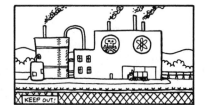

PAN/ZOOM TO:

A drain pipe spewing foul ooze into a nearby marsh.

---

CUT TO CLOSE-UP:

Bubbles.

Music builds as we see...

...a greenish hand emerge from the vile and disgusting pool of slime!!!

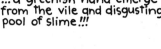

CRANE SHOT:

Out of the goo it rises... a creature born from toxic sludge... a monster whose name would become synonymous with doom!!!

---

Music crescendos.

Roll title.

THE PAIGE FOX STORY

JASON, I'M BUSY. WHY DON'T YOU ASK PAIGE TO PROOFREAD YOUR SCREENPLAY?

UM...